COLOR THE WILD
NATIONAL PARKS
COLORING BOOK FOR ADULTS

THANK YOU!
For choosing this coloring book

We are thrilled that you have decided to embark on a colorful journey through the magnificent landscapes and stunning natural wonders of the national parks of America. By choosing our book, you are not only supporting our small business but also helping to preserve and protect these iconic locations for future generations to enjoy. We hope that as you color your way through the pages, you will feel a sense of awe and wonder at the breathtaking beauty of these parks and that the experience will inspire you to explore and appreciate the great outdoors.

This coloring book features 63 pages of illustrations, each one capturing the unique essence and spirit of a different national park. Whether you're an experienced artist or just starting out, our coloring book offers hours of relaxation and creative expression.

Please note: we highly recommend that you use colored pencils or crayons. That will give you the best overall coloring experience and make some beautiful and amazing finished pieces. If you do decide to use paint or markers, then be sure to put a blank piece of paper behind your drawing to avoid any bleed-through!

NOW!
stay calm and color

Acadia National Park

American Samoa National Park

Arches National Park

Badlands National Park

Big Bend National Park

Biscayne National Park

Black Canyon of the Gunnison National Park

Bryce Canyon National Park

Canyonlands National Park

Capitol Reef National Park

Carlsbad Caverns National Park

Channel Islands National Park

Congaree National Park

Crater Lake National Park

Cuyahoga Valley National Park

Death Valley National Park

Denali National Park and Preserve

Dry Tortugas National Park

Everglades National Park

Gates of the Arctic National Park and Preserve

Gateway Arch National Park

Glacier Bay National Park and Preserve

Glacier National Park

Grand Canyon National Park

Grand Teton National Park

Great Basin National Park

Great Sand Dunes National Park and Preserve

Great Smoky Mountains National Park

Guadalupe Mountains National Park

Haleakalā National Park

Hawai'i Volcanoes National Park

Hot Springs National Park

Indiana Dunes National Park

Isle Royale National Park

Joshua Tree National Park

Katmai National Park and Preserve

Kenai Fjords National Park

Kings Canyon National Park

Kobuk Valley National Park

Lake Clark National Park and Preserve

Lassen Volcanic National Park

Mammoth Cave National Park

Mesa Verde National Park

Mount Rainier National Park

New River Gorge National Park and Preserve

North Cascades National Park

Olympic National Park

Petrified Forest National Park

Pinnacles National Park

Redwood National and State Parks

Rocky Mountain National Park

Saguaro National Park

Sequoia National Park

Shenandoah National Park

Theodore Roosevelt National Park

Virgin Islands National Park

Voyageurs National Park

White Sands National Park

Wind Cave National Park

Wrangell-St. Elias National Park and Preserve

Yellowstone National Park

Yosemite National Park

Zion National Park

Made in the USA
Coppell, TX
07 June 2023